Read Me

Victoria Guzman

Read Me

Copyright © 2024 by Victoria Guzman.

All rights reserved. No part of this publication may be reproduced, distributed, or transmitted in any form or by any means, including photocopying, recording, or other electronic or mechanical methods, without the written consent of the publisher. The only exceptions are for brief quotations included in critical reviews and other noncommercial uses permitted by copyright law.

This publication contains the author's personal thoughts and viewpoints. It is intended to provide helpful and informative material on the topics addressed in the book. It is important to note that utilizing any of the contents within may carry some degree of liability, loss, or risk—be it personal or otherwise. The author and publisher explicitly disclaim any responsibility, whether direct or indirect, for such outcomes.

MILTON & HUGO L.L.C.
4407 Park Ave., Suite 5
Union City, NJ 07087, USA

Website: *www.miltonandhugo.com*
Hotline: *1-888-778-0033*
Email: *info@miltonandhugo.com*

Ordering Information:
Quantity sales. Special discounts are granted to corporations, associations, and other organizations. For more information on these discounts, please reach out to the publisher using the contact information provided above.

Library of Congress Control Number:	2024923222	
ISBN-13:	979-8-89285-305-7	[Paperback Edition]
	979-8-89285-304-0	[Digital Edition]

Rev. date: 10/30/2024

Introduction

Read Me

I will give you my stories
Without saying a word
When I stand in front of you just read me
My eyes, lips, and body
Have words all over them
You just have to look closely to see
Where the pencil left its markings.

Where I am From...

I am from scratched glasses, from dull pencils, and used notebooks.
I am from the damaged roads and a small brick home.
I am from the backyard smell of being a kid and getting dirty;
From scraping my knees and going where my imagination took me.
I am from sharing with my sisters and showing my support.
I am from riding bikes and getting soaked in the rain with my family.
From "You'll be fine", "Love yourself"
I'm from the cross and bible, and from a growing church.
I'm from a hospital room.
From my mother's pain and from her direction.
From the time we got our first puppy and the time I got my first friend.
I am from that white laced album with pink ribbon
That's in the broken purple box filled with pictures up in the closet, and my black drawer...
Filled with times I wasn't around and pictures of real people, and filled with letters and drawings.
All showing captured seconds that are only a part of me.
I am from my past and my present memories.

That Little Girl

I wear sixteen years
My experiences, my memories
Wrap around me like a sweater
I am still growing
In September I will have seventeen years on me
A young woman
Or young lady
That's what you see
But remember I wear all the years
On my sleeves
I am still that baby that was in my mother's arms
I am still that baby that stole my mother's heart
That toddler that took a step and fell
I got back up
I started walking
I am still walking
That was me as well
That little girl that was happy
Reality did not consume her
She smiled
She knew joy and joked around
That was me
I was that child
I still joke, maybe in a different way
I still laugh and grin, maybe not every day
I am growing
Maturing
I am that little girl
Just not scared of the dark
I fear something much deeper

I know life can be hard
I am that little girl
I still have my teddy bear
But I don't really need it
So it's on my bed just sitting there
I am still that little girl with a halo above her head
But now it's gone and I'm growing wings instead
I am still that kid that jumped on a trampoline and thought
"I can fly"
I know better now
I learned with time
That kid that jumped in the leaves
That kid that always tripped over her own two feet
That little girl that played in the rain
Then I jumped when the thunder came
I am that five-year-old that made mud pies
I wear sixteen years
They're all mine
Even when I'm eighty
And I have wrinkles on my skin
I will be wearing all my years
Even at eighty, I will still be that kid
Right now
I wear sixteen years
I am still me at any age
A book keeps its title even when you turn the page
Each chapter in my life
Or however long I'm in this world
I am me and I am still that little girl

Skin

Skin, that is what I have
Wrapped around my bones and muscles
It can be protection
It can mask my thoughts and troubles
But it is not steel
It can display my weaknesses and wounds
Sticks and stones
Can cause pain and leave me very bruised
My skin covers me
It's a wall, a thick barrier, a barricade
It goes all around me
And it is a blanket to hide my heart away
No one is allowed
To see passed or peak under
What would they think
Of the color of my blood, I wonder?
If you get the chance
Touch it gently, don't press too hard
It is tough, but
I still fear you will leave a mark

Innocence

I feel as if though I'm a child and my eyes are being opened
Opened to the world's true colors
The earth is brown, the sky is blue, the grass is green
But I'm looking passed that
I'm looking closer
I can see a darker side
Black where a shadow lays on the ground
Gray where the sky cries
Dingy purple where someone is bruised
Before I had a filter on my eyes and mind
My hand was held
So I couldn't walk further
My eyes were shut
So I would be kept from the truth
I was told monsters don't exist
And families are supposed to be happy
I was told I would never be alone and the sun will rise again
But maybe I was lied to
Because there are bad guys and daddy made mommy cry
Because I was left alone outside in the cold
And the hands on the clock can stop turning
I turned away from the fairytale stories
There are not always happily ever afters
The villain doesn't always get caught
And people can be ignorant and selfish
It is like stepping into a new light
Where the sun burns my skin
It is like I'm a blank white piece of paper
Now stained by black ink
It is like a scar from a blade that cut so deep,

it is displayed and it is not going to go away
Years are passing and I am growing
I have learned to not be afraid
To not be intimidated by the world
To not expect a happy ending
It is okay to know the truth
But I should have taken advantage of my youth
Maybe I found out a little too soon.

Sometimes

I need to go back
Erase my mind from all the knowledge that I have
I need to go back to coloring outside the lines
Back to chasing butterflies and picking dandelions
Back to running on the playground
And hanging from the monkey bars
Back to laying on the grass and looking up at the stars
Back to finger painting and catching fireflies
Oh, how those were simpler times
I want to go back to playing make believe
I love creating my own reality
Stress and sadness do not exist
Neither does doubt nor loneliness
Sometimes the world can be overwhelming
An escape would be nice
I just need to breathe
I just need to take a step back sometimes

Tigress

I'm a caged tiger at the zoo
Looking at glass I can't get through
People glance, then walk right by
No getting out, I'm trapped inside
Pacing, pacing back and forth
I don't know what lies ahead or what I'm headed towards
My audience only sees what I look like
They don't see passed these black stripes
And under my thick soft fur
They don't see me clearly; I'm just a blur

Things I Can't Buy

I went into a store...
So much to buy, and not enough money to spend.
Picked out a few things, but let me think it over again.
A floral or plain blouse, or long or short dress.
I really don't want anything from here I guess.
I want all the things you can't buy
I want the things that aren't in the store, things you can't find
How much will it cost to buy that smile on your face?
Where can I buy joy and true happiness? Where? What place?
What about a thin body? What is the cost to be content with myself?
Can I buy a new prettier face? Instead of that make-up on the shelf?
Can I buy a mirror that shows a better reflection?
Does it cost a million dollars to buy perfection?
Tell me where to buy a clock that goes slow, and gives me time.
Who has the best life? How much to call that life mine?
Where can I buy confidence, and what is the price?
What about honesty? How much would it cost for someone to tell the truth, no lies?
Is it expensive? Intelligence? Where can I get a better brain?
Do I have to pay to get attention, though, I am not talking about fame?
There are so many things I want to buy; just tell me where to go.
These things will lift me up and help me not feel so low.
One last request...
How much for someone else's personality?
How much will it cost to be someone better than me?

A New Day

I wake up
Eyes puffy from the tears of yesterday's...
Loss,
Hurt,
And pain.
I'm sad, but the sky looks happy
There are no gray clouds, nor rain.
I get out of bed and step on the floor.
It feels different
Did it feel this way before?
That is not the only thing new...
This is a new morning, a new day without you

A Picture

The sound of your voice,
The smell on your shirt,
The joy in your smile,
The look on your face...
When you saw me.
A picture of you in my memory,
And in my mind.
Even though you are gone.

Shooting Star

I saw a shooting star in the sky
or maybe it was just a firefly
It doesn't matter, I made a wish...

I wished for a smile that is sincere
I wished that all the sadness would disappear
I wished everyone felt that they belong
I wished people would do the right thing not the wrong
I wished people weren't all alone
I wished people had a place to call home
I wished everyone felt loved
I know not everyone gets enough
I wished no one would starve
I wished life wasn't so hard
I wished there weren't feelings so low,
But then again those feelings help us learn and grow
I wished everyone could have delight
I wished there was only a bright side
I wished everyone would care
I wished that life wasn't so unfair
I wished there wasn't depression
I wished there was such thing as perfection
I wished there was more time
I wished everything would be fine

This is probably a hard wish to make come true
So why try, what's the use?
I'll have hope...
What if the star has more power than meets the eye?
What if all we need is that shooting star in the sky?

Suffocation

Air
That's what I need
Remove your hands from my neck
Loosen your grip
Let me breathe
You know what?
Just leave them there
Better yet hold on tighter
Suffocate me
Let life escape from my body

Let Me Rest

I'm tired, my eyes keep wanting to close
But I keep them open
People around me don't know
how hard it is to be awake
My eyelids are weights
So heavy, my mind aches
I just want to sleep, life has kept me up
Late at night into the morning
I'm done
I need my bed
My pillows
Let me rest
Let me fall and land on something soft
I just want a break, a few minutes
No, a few days off
Someone take my legs and walk for me
Someone use my brain and think for me
My energy is gone
This day is draining
It is dragging on and on
Seconds feel like hours, they're taking too long
Someone just take my body, leave my soul to rest
Leave it alone
I'm too tired
To walk, to blink
To breathe, to speak
I'd rather not be here
I'm just going to lay
And rest my mind
I'm not going to dream
Don't wake me
I'll be fine

Anything but Human

I don't want to be human
I'm tired of walking in the same body
I'm tired of wearing my skin
Can I be something else?
I wouldn't mind being the break of dawn
Waking the day
Or the sunrise
Filling the sky with colors
I would like to be the smell of coffee in the morning
Being the reason someone gets out of bed
It would be exciting being a flower
Or a gift to give to a loved one
I would be valued
Or music, yes music
I want to be the notes played from a piano
I want to be the strings of a guitar
I want to be the melody that someone hums
Or a peaceful tune from a harp
I want to feed souls
Or can I be the hands of a child
That you don't want to let go of
I should be food
That's something people love
The flavors on someone's tongue
Keeping someone's tummy satisfied
Can I be the lips that smile on a face
Or gleaming eyes
No, the sun rays that peek through the clouds
Better yet, I want to be thunder
I want people to hear a glorious sound

I want to be pouring rain
Soaking the ground
Watering seeds
I want to be the wind
I want to be a warm summer breeze
Can I be a canvas
Or paint?
Can I be someone's masterpiece?
I want to be something special
Something unique
Something that people find astounding
Or even a dandelion seed
Someone make a wish upon me
Can I be dopamine released in someone's brain
I want to be love
Not loved, love
I want to be the butterflies when hands touch
I want to be a roller coaster
Giving people that rush
A thrilling feeling
I want to be something
Other than a human being
I want to be the sky
Or a birds wing
I want to be something greater than me
The sea
I want to be an ocean's tide
I want to be a star
I want to be moonlight
I want to be something
Better than myself
Not human
I want to be something else
Even if it's just a rose petal
Or a sweater

Or even a wall
I don't mind being a white winter
Or colorful fall
Anything
I want to be anything at all
Even ink in a pen
I want to be anything
Anything but human

Torn

At times I feel pinned down
Legs numb
Making it impossible to stand
My arms held down
Not letting me up
My mouth sewn
Shut
Not letting my words escape
Not letting me holler
And my vision is blurred
Without my glasses
At times I feel helpless
I'm in a frozen state
In a vulnerable place
Fingers
They not only touch
They dig
To deep
Inflicting pain
And it feels like
My w o r l d
Is being
t o r n a p a r t

Every Now and Then

I'm hung up on the old you
Wondering where the man I fell in love with went
And you reach out to hold me and fix me to become the women who isn't me yet
I look in your eyes to find you before you did what you did
And I stand before you giving you my best and it's not enough to just live
There has been misunderstandings and a long tug of war
We can't change the past. We can only grieve what we can't say sorry for
There's hope in our eyes, hoping for better tomorrow's and that the other still cares
We want it to work, we love hard and deep. I still think we are the perfect pair

WANTED

I let you go further than anybody else before
I let you in.
I displayed myself
Felt like a picture in a frame
Or a painting on a wall
But a picture frame can end up on the floor
Broken
Glass scattered everywhere
And a painting can be ruined
Stained
Or even torn apart
I felt like a flower
A single flower in a garden
Left uncared for
Ended up wilting
I let you see me
Because you made me feel
Wanted
I let your hand slip further
South
Sliding down my back
Or up my leg
Despite my mind telling me to
Get away or the letters
N O
Held on my tongue
Because your hands felt
As if you actually cared
And your fingers felt like you were
Writing

Wanted
ALL over me
I ignored your eyes wondering when we spoke
And the demand in your voice
I should have known
That you only cared for
Yourself
Your pleasure
And you only wanted my body
You never wanted me

Waiting

I was waiting for my curbside to be filled with a parked car
I was waiting for a car door to be shut after you got out
I was waiting for your knuckle to hit my door so you could be let in
I was wait for you
To come to me

I was waiting for you to say you were wrong
I was waiting for you to stop me from shaking my head
I was waiting for you to step closer and comfort me
I was waiting for the space to be closed between us
I was waiting for you
To hold me

I was waiting on a fantasy, something that only could happen in a book
I was waiting because I held on to hope and your memory
I was waiting on something impossible, I was waiting on a dream
I was waiting for a day that you realized you are better with me
I was waiting for you
To want me

I stopped waiting for the sound of your car outside my house
I stopped waiting on an eager knock at my door
I stopped waiting for your arms to wrap around me
I stopped waiting to be held by you and
I stopped waiting to hear apologetic words
Because it wasn't going to happen

I stopped waiting on you
To come to me
To want me
And hold Me

No more waiting
It's pointless
You're not worth
Waiting on
If you don't see my worth
You don't deserve me

I Don't Mean To

I don't mean to
But I feel like you'll move on
Like if I'm an old sweater
That you'll get tired of wearing
Or a pair of shoes
That will end up unseen
In the back of your closet
I feel like you'll get tired,
Irritated,
Fed up with me
I don't mean to
Have these negative thoughts,
But people move on
People can walk away
People can leave
Me standing alone wondering
What did I do?
Was it something I said?
People have left me
Thinking I'm not enough
I don't mean to
Think you think the same,
But the thought has crossed my mind
Because you can abandon me
Like a house
That had a family
Then they moved out
Leaving that house empty
Tell me what I can do to
Stay fresh on your mind

And not get lost in your memory
I don't mean to
Feel like a favorite song
That you can play over and over
Until you turn it off
And move on to a
New rhythm
New melody
You can let me know
When
You feel I'm not the best company
I don't mean to
Let these thoughts race
Let you down
I don't mean to
But these thoughts may be
Already pushing you away

Double Edged

I hid the blade with a loving smile
And a welcoming hug
I stabbed you
Over a dozen of times
You only thought I was coming in for a hug
It's like your eyes ignored the sharp silver
Blade headed straight for you
You bled after it dug in deeper than a few inches
By the time it appeared out of your
Back, you gave me a look
There was pain screaming for help
But I also heard your heart beat
For me
A whisper
I still love you
The wound will be there to stay
As will I and embrace every smile of yours
 I look at you, for you are so beautiful
And I will look down and the blood never washed off my hands
We keep it
The pain, the lies
All in our memories
No one knows better than us, nothing cuts deeper than a lie

I'll Never Understand

When did we become enemies?
When did he become the prize?
Why are you to blame?
Wait, why am I?
When did it all start?
When was the first lie?
When did yall meet?
When was the first night?
When did you find out?
When was the first fight?
When did he say he loves you
After he kissed me Goodnight?
When did he convince you
That you were the only one in his eyes?
He gave me the same
Old lovely twisted lies.
Why did you not warn me?
Why did you take his side?
You knew the truth all along.
That we were sharing the same guy.
Why did you think you could make him stay?
Even I couldn't, no matter how hard I tried.
He'd kiss me on the cheek
But you'd be on his mind.
I seen another name on his phone
I'd seen the signs
I wanted to believe those three words.
I was hopelessly blind.
I thought it was me. I just
Needed to be more loving and kind.

Did you know it wasn't us?
It was him, he wouldn't ever be satisfied.
Why did you let him win,
Thinking he'd choose you at the finish line?
He'd choose himself unaware
That I am the prize.
We are not enemies
He's to blame, not you or I
The truth hurts, and my heart hurts even more, but it'll heal. Give it time.
You deserve better than
Those meaningless little pick up lines
Don't betray yourself, you know what to do.
Learn, grow, and live your life.

All of Me

I was waiting for others
To see how valuable I am
Or if I had any at all
Without knowing it I
Convinced myself I had none
I didn't even see it leave me
It was just never there
In the first place
That would explain their response
What do you want?
MORE
Even after I had scrubbed the floors
And alphabetized the DVDs
There was always more to do
Never time to sit
No time to rest
Let alone breathe
Then there was you
You were different
You wanted all of me
More of my love
More of my mind
More of my thoughts
More of my time
I was scared of letting you in
Giving you more
I had already given so much
I was worried I wouldn't be enough
Or maybe I'd be too much
Because no one has ever wanted that much
Of me

But you said to give it all to you
I was hesitant at first
It took a while to come out of my shell
But I'm out now
And you're tired of my thoughts
They are to negative
You're tired of my habits
Tired off hearing about my day
You don't know how hard it was
To learn how to tell you about all the details
It's like twisting a towel that was soaked
And trying to get every drop of water out
But when I said my day was good
You wanted more
So I gave it all to you
I gave myself up little by little
Not knowing what the limit was
Was I supposed to have one?
I'd give up all my time
All my energy
You could have it
All
It wasn't until I was bleeding
That I thought that it may be unhealthy
It wasn't until I was ready to even give up my life
That I thought maybe I shouldn't rely on
Others
Approval
"Value" measurements
Other's wants
I want more than to be a puppet
I'll cut the strings and try to be more
Not for any one else
Just for me

People Pleaser

I can tell you want you want to hear
I can show you what you want to see
I can blend in in the background
I can mingle in the crowd
I can be a friend to lean on
I can keep my head low and shut my mouth
I can sit and look ready for whatever is next
I can be what you need me to be
Or at the very least I'll try my best

Unlearning What was Taught

Who am I
If I've only ever been living for everybody else?
It's not unheard of to be young
And not know yourself
I got the people pleaser gene
Don't take up space, quiet down, go unseen

Being emotional was never a crime
I wish I knew that growing up
I'm barely learning who I was
And who I want to be
That I am *Enough*
Then again, the mothers before me didn't know
they didn't have to swallow the lump in their throat
or quiet down their laugh
I didn't have to go through it all alone
I could have gotten help, I just had to ask

I'll start a new chapter, a new lesson
There aren't limits, no cage to be kept in
I'm a woman, not a word to fit your definition
The only one leading me will be God, he's my direction

Another Step Forward

I love seeing that small light in the distance.
The one at the end of the tunnel.
It's so dark, and it gives me a little more energy to take another step forward
But sometimes it feels like the Tunnel is endless
Almost a mind game
Waiting for me to give up, wondering how long I'll keep going
How long can it torture me?
How long will I let it drag on, and when will I accept my fate?
It will run me into insanity

Victim Mentality

I've never been raped
But I've been stripped with eyes
That feel so uncomfortable
My goosebumps rise
And peel my skin back
Making me feel more bare
And ashamed to be just breathing
Even though I shouldn't be
I've not been physically abused
Thank God
But words have given me wounds I'm still healing from
Words that penetrated so deep
A bullet would be easier to dig out with my fingers
Than trying to get to them
I haven't been shot
But my hope is bleeding out
And my heart is turning colder
No pressure can stop the pain
I've never had a loved one die
Maybe it's me who's dying
On the inside, wait for my time
Or just dying to live
And find someone
That's living in me and
Wants to breathe
I've never had anything bad
Happen to me
Nothing worth telling
Life is just running its course
For everybody

Sometimes I Feel Like the Rain

Sometimes I feel like the rain
Dreary
Bits of me fading away
Losing myself

Sometimes I feel like the rain
A source for people
Hydrating the earth
Helping flowers bloom

Sometimes I feel like the rain
Powerful
Causing ripples in puddles
Or flooding streets

Sometimes I feel like the rain
Glorious
But not everyone
Sees it the same

Sometimes I feel like the rain
Dull
Dark
Gloomy and gray

Sometimes I feel like the rain
Unappreciated
Giving so much
In the end
Drained

Rainy day

I'm walking through the rain,
water all around
Surrounded by that pounding
booming sound
Heavy droplets weighing me down
darkness fills my mind
The outcome of the gray skies
absence of light
Can you see it through my eyes?

Rumors

The wind
Listens then
Spreads the word
It shifts
And becomes
Louder than a whisper

Twisting and turning
The truth
So fast
Can't tell
How long the
Truth will last

Sometimes it is
Nothing more than
A light breeze
Or it can be
A tornado and damage
Is what it leaves

Whether it spreads
Joy or negativity
No matter what
The wind blows
Wild and free

Titanic

Sometimes words feel like the tip of an iceberg
when it comes to describing heartache.
the grief is so much deeper

Taking in Moments

Artwork

Inside a building of people's creations
My eyes are drawn to a spectrum of colors and intricate sculptures,
Yet I have seen more astounding pieces of art.
Don't get me wrong, I admire the effort, time, and skill that the artists have.
However, they cannot compare to God's work. He created man; our lungs, heads and our hearts.

Who has mastered painting people's skin?
Down to a blue vain across an arm
Or the deepest darkest brown in an eye
With the lashes framing a person's perspective
Who has created something that perfectly captures the essence of beauty or
True joy. The lord has made the colors and symbols of love.
For he has constructed a beating heart. And has shown affection.

He went down to the furthest detail, putting wrinkles in my hands.
It is like he has drawn out a map that I can grasp.
His art grows from the past and is about the present, but leans towards the future.
He created a guide.
Not only did he design a person's face and figure, but also a living space.
With his hands, he built the crust. The rich soil for life to be planted.
The rough, rugged mountainous rocks.
And the texture of the water in the ocean's tide.

The audible sounds of everyday life also originated from him.
A calm voice that says hello, a mockingbird's song, the wind's whistle, or the song of a whale
All sprung from him, but there is more.

The sky is his canvas painted blue, pink, orange, yellow, at different times of the day.
Leaving white fuzzy layers of clouds or he paints it gray.
With sun rays trying to peek through.
He flashes light and bangs the drums while letting water hit the floor.

He went further than creating this atmosphere.
Have you not noticed the bright balls of gas in the sky?
Haven't you heard of other universes?
Sure, outer space can be seen as a mystery, but that is the beauty of his work.

The roots that dive into the ground to the highest leaf.
The depths of the oceans to the tallest mountain.
Then beyond the stars. God's creations are perfectly imperfect.
Even crooked smiles and tilted trees are beautiful.
He made this world with love and compassion. Every detail. Every aspect.

No one can measure up to his creations. He created everything and everyone around me.
He created this whole world and universe. He has created a masterpiece.

Beachy Keen

Sand in between my toes
Dry then there the water goes
The scent of salt and sand
I was in love
With the sun going down
Colors reflecting on the ocean
Beauty all around
First excitement and overjoyed
The feeling of freedom washes over me
My breath is taken away
By the sight of the sea
And the moment of this glorious day

Backyard Adventures

We open the backdoor, while opening our minds. Letting it run wild, with thoughts and ideas. Of where we will go and play. Where we will Explore. Discovering new territories that we haven't seen before. Behind that tree lies a dragon, a dangerous beast. Only disguised as our puppy. The branches move. But it wasn't because of the wind. It moved to say hi. The tree is our friend. We look around for weapons. To scare the dragon off. Our friend, the tree provides them. Our swords, bows, and arrows. We forget about the wild beast and set up camp. Our minds are everywhere. We pick up sticks while getting dirt in our nails without a care. We are young adventures. We build a fire and make up stories. Having the time of our camper lives. But all of it comes to an end. Mama bear calls us in. because the sun has to rest. To make a new day tomorrow so we can come out again. To explore. Maybe we will touch the sky? Tomorrow we will jump on the trampoline to fly. Or we will dig up a treasure. No matter what, when that backdoor opens, We will create our own adventure.

Why Remember My Name?

I passed by you before
Our eyes met for a second
I heard your voice
Friendly and pleasant

We cross paths a few
Times throughout the week
But I didn't think I caught
Your eye, I didn't think you remembered me

When you spoke
Your words directed at me
This is new, unfamiliar
A little surprising

Then you said it; you called
Me by name so casually
Like you saved it and
Finally released it from your memory

Until that moment, I didn't
think you knew of my existence
I didn't think you saw me
Nor did I think you listened

how you speak to me...

Silence. I look around the room; letting my eyes
Run wild until I see your lips turn upwards. Happy
To see me? Seeing your smile, that's what I'm reading.
Squeezing my hand tighter, you don't want to let go.
Watching the time, hoping it moves slow.
When we say goodbye, it seems like you don't want
To leave. You linger. You take one last look at me.
Don't have to say anything at all.
Your mouth can speak, but your body also talks.

F-A-M-I-L-Y

Family is a label people wear when they share the same blood.

Or it's deeper. Their souls connect. There's mutual respect and love.

Family is an excuse to walk all over someone. To betray and return.

It's used as a promise that you'll stay even after being burned.

To ask for an arm and a leg and expect you to keep walking.

It's an interruption when you want to be heard, but someone else keeps talking

Family can be your last hope when you feel lonely and abandoned

They can be a call away. Your ride home when you are lost or stranded.

Family can be your definition of drama, the opposite of peace.

But it can also be your saving grace, when you're locked out they have a back up key

It can be used as an excuse to be forgiven

And other times they are the people that make life worth living

They can be the ones who pull your hair and call you names

Or they are people you lean on when there are heavier days

It is a title not always made from blood,

They are people we choose, people we trust, people we love

It's Simple

Nurture me
Cherish me
Hold my hand
I don't just let anyone stand
Beside me
And call them
My one and only
Don't step back and leave me lonely.

Open Door

It scares me
Showing you my life
My thoughts
My tears
My bruises
But also
My happiness
My true smiles
Letting you in
Opening the door bit by bit
I am welcoming you
Now you can walk inside
Some of the rooms are locked
But they'll open with time
But I won't let fear
Block you from walking further
Because it is scary
Displaying myself
Like a picture frame on the wall
Or art in a gallery
But what scares me more
Is not knowing you at all
Not having you in my life
Not spending time with you
Making memories
That I will never forget
Not feeling your arm around me
Or feeling your embrace
Not hearing those words
From your mouth

Not knowing that look in your eyes
So I'll let you in
Maybe not all at once
But at least you got inside

Autumn

The trees sway back and forth
Celebrating that autumn has finally arrived
My hands are ice and the wind blows cold
I never felt so alive

The wind gains power
Each day grows colder
The scenery gives me inspiration
For some reason, I feel braver and bolder

I stand outside shivering,
But I choose to stay
I admire the dying plants
And the beautiful colors they display

I think back on the day
When I jumped in the leaf pile
We were laughing
And we played for a while

So I will stand here
even though my sweater is to thin
To hear the winds whistle and see the colors
and to take it all in
Because time doesn't rest
and pretty soon this season will end

Winter

She says hello
When the wind blows
Blows my hair out of my face
Blows my eyes shut
Blows my sweater open

She says hello
By saying goodbye to the leaves
Falling off the branches
Falling on the dry grass
Falling because they don't have the strength to hold on
Falling where I step, then crumbles to pieces

She says hello
With someone putting on a scarf
Putting up the tree
Putting the heater on
Putting boots on their feet
Putting snow as a blanket for the ground

She says hello
While I try to get warm
Get closer to others
Get shivers down my spine
Get goosebumps all over my arms
Get inside away from her

She says hello
But she does not intend on staying
Intend on icing the roads
Intend on bringing people close

Intend on being so captivating
Intend on making you miss her

She says hello
But has to say goodbye
Has to move on
Has to go

Thunderstorm

Gray clouds covering the sky
Giving the sun a place to hide
The sound of an abrupt boom echoes
Then a light flashes by

Windows and walls shaking and
Trees moving side to side
A thunderstorm is dark
And *one of the most beautiful things in life.*

At the end of the day,
It won't be the money spent
Nor the materials bought
That runs through my mind
It will be the smiles and laughs,
The way you held me
And treated me
So sweet and so kind

- Thanks for all the memories were making

When I grow up...

What do you want to be when you grow up?
I get asked this often enough.
They expect a career I'm interested in,
But let me think the question over again...
I want to be a hard worker that people notice;
Someone that can be fun and also have focus.
I want to be someone that others look up to.
I want to be an example of dreams coming true.
I want to be somebody that is fearless and brave;
Someone that doesn't look back and is unafraid.
I want to be relentless; someone who puts up a fight.
I will work hard, then harder to do all things right.
I want to be proud when I look at my reflection,
Even with my flaws and imperfections.
I don't want to be ideal
I want to be someone who keeps their composure, despite what they feel.
I want to be known, by at least a few or by the nation,
For my greatness. I want to be an inspiration.
I want to be someone that is strong without a doubt.
I want to be... Well, I don't have it all figured out.

Encouragement

You try your best and give it your all
Still, you fail, but get up from your fall
You are back at it, running full speed
Passing others, now taking the lead
Then you trip and stumble
You need help, you're in trouble
You're hurt, but still, you get up
You wonder "will I ever be good enough?"
Ignore the doubt, keep on moving
Persevere even when you're losing
Never give up, never give in
Keep trying, keep working until the end

Moving Forward

Imperfection and mistakes
are made often
A word is all it takes
a friendship has fallen

Then again many things break,
things you can't fix
so many problems
Doing all it takes
just to solve them

Wait?! Isn't today a new day?
Shouldn't yesterday be forgotten?
Shouldn't I feel fine or okay?
not guilty, selfish, or rotten?...

Yes, that is true!!!
It is a new day!
I should stop feeling blue
and find a new way

So I'll say goodbye
to….
the regretful,
the hurtful,
the shameful,
and the unpleasant memories
My mind has to be set free
from all that negativity

Now that I have that weight off my shoulders
I will walk with my head held high
My past is no longer my controller
All because I said…

Bye…
Bye...
Bye…

Redemption

Everyone is different and at the same time
We are all the same
We all grow up and we all change
We smile, laugh, and we cry
We learn, love, and we lie
And at some point, we get caught up in meaningless things
And we lose ourselves,
we lose our personalities
The person we used to be gets replaced
The person we used to be hides away,
But deep down they're in there somewhere
There is not a map you can use to find them
and there is not a guide
It is all up to you to find who you truly are inside
Or find a better version of you
We can't be who everyone wants us to be
There will always be someone unhappy
That is the world we live in
It is hard, but we need to accept ourselves
And learn from the difficult times
And not get trapped by negativity
You are free
Be who *you* want to be
Look on the brighter side of things
Each day is a new opportunity
To be better
To be stronger
To redeem yourselves
Let your cheeks lift, and your eyes gleam,
just smile

Focus on the things that are worth your while
Let those sad and lonely feelings be gone
Because the sun will set and a new day will dawn

What to Be...

There are many things to be
Be strong, crazy, and free
Be beautiful and wondrous
Be wonderful and victorious
Be courageous and brave
Be humble and respectful
And behave
Be big and bold
Be kind, but don't get controlled
Be fierce and fast
Be first, not last
Be diligent and engaged
Be you don't change
Be real, not fake
Be different, it's ok
Be joyous and ecstatic
Be outstanding and fantastic
Be lovable and caring
Be outgoing and daring
Be a dreamer
Be an artist
Be a creative thinker
Be persistent
Be you, no one else
Be confident
Be yourself

Just Luck

Is that what you call my victory?
Luck?
Is it because it was unexpected or was it jealousy?
Maybe it was luck
If luck is taking the time to improve
And working hard
If luck is refusing to take a break
Even when I can't catch my breath
If luck is giving it my all
Every drop of sweat
Maybe some tears
If luck is taking the pain and pushing through
If luck is accomplishing my goals
If luck is being dedicated
If luck going back at it
Even after failing miserably
Even after a bit of doubt being put in my head
If luck is tackling every obstacle in my way
Fighting to succeed
If luck is resilience
If luck is be ready to go even further
If luck is an ambitious mindset
If luck is something you earn
If luck is testing the limits and pushing boundaries
If luck has any correlation to any of this
Then yes
I guess that's what it is
Just luck

Life is Temporary

Treasured Times

When you were around
Moments passed slow
Where did they go?

It was a flash
Now looking back
But I'm happy for the time we did have

The funny, stressful, and joyous memories
Are kept within me forever
Remembered and kept as a treasure

Just Thinking

It is late and everyone has shut their eyes
But my eyes won't close no matter how hard I try
So I look out my window, out to the dark night sky
And I think of how today is about to be yesterday and how time flies

I lay still, and listen to my watch's rhythm
Maybe it will put me to sleep
So I continue to listen while tapping along to the continuous beat
It's no use, my mind won't rest, so I guess I will stay up and think

My mind goes back through my memory, not any particular day
Back to the time when we shared laughter while getting soaked in the rain
Back to when things were too good to be true, times of cliché
I treasure those memories, I will never let them slip away

I remember times of struggle and hurt, my life isn't perfect
I can't undo mistakes or rewrite my past, I have no regrets
I won't ignore what's happened, the ups and downs are too hard to forget
I learned and grew stronger, my passed has built me up I guess

It feels like so much has happened in such little time
I will cherish every second, minute, hour, and day that I can call mine
Now I'll fall asleep so sound, so gratified
I was just thinking and just thinking can keep me up all night

The Clock

I don't want this feeling, this moment to end. I don't want to say goodbye.
I'm going to close my eyes and squeeze my fist, maybe if I hold tight enough
Maybe then, the clock won't spin. It's no use, the clock is still ticking. I guess
There is not a remote to press pause, but If I could hold on to a moment for a
Few more seconds, it would be for a good cause. May I stop it once, just to look
Around? So I can take in every scent, color, movement, and sound. Until that
Miracle happens, I will watch time pass and always see a bright side and reach
For happiness if it is in my grasp.

Time

Time doesn't have wings, but it flies by
A clock has hands,
but you can't hold on to a moment for too long
Time isn't money, it is memories
Time includes numbers, but you can't count on it
There is no specific time though
There are several time zones
Good morning and goodnight
Time is confusing
Time is not infinite
It will end
The time is now and
It is a privilege
Taken for granted

Patient End

Whether laughter is released, or a fight occurs
The sun may set one last time
Whether a problem gets resolved or not
The sun may not feel like giving earth another day
It doesn't matter if we got out of bed or wasted the day away
That could be the last morning, noon, and night
The last chance to inhale a deep breath
The last time we walked around
And saw the world
The streets busy or empty
People smiling, together, just living
It could be the last time of having your first kiss
Or first anything
The sun could just go down
Even after a stormy day
Or a flood
Of tears, or hurt
It doesn't really matter
If there is satisfaction of how the day was spent
Or how the week went
Or what anyone went through
No matter what we learned or how we grew
Up to be or if there is an infant
That didn't get to live at all.
The sun may not rise again
This day could be our last
This could be the end

Patient End Part 2

Death could come to our doorstep and knock
Matter a fact
It could walk right in, it has that power
Though the knock wouldn't be heard
There wouldn't be a creek when the door opened
No warning, no sign
It would just step inside
And it would just be

The end
Of your life.

Patient End Final Part

Maybe it's not as patient as it seems
It can take anyone
At anytime
In the middle of a breath
In the middle of a meal
In the middle of a conversation
In the middle of a road trip
In the middle of a blizzard
In the middle of the night
An interruption
No a halt
Unexpected
It is like the fingers that pinch
A candle's lit end
It puts out the flame
Unaware of the person's
Family, memories, or their name
It is like the switch to the light
But when it goes off
No way to switch it back on
Snaps its fingers
Another funeral to attend
It's untimely
A not so patient end

Legacy

If the sun's rays that peek through my windows
were not loud enough to wake me. If my eyes
did not meet the morning and did not get to see
the day. If my feet left the ground untouched,
and the dirt lonely. If my hands never waved
hello or shook a stranger's hand again. Instead
they waved goodbye without knowing for the
last time. If I was swept from this universe.

How would people take it, my presence gone.
My smile not to be seen again. Or any expression
on my face or body, for that matter. My mouth
silent, not another word to be spoken. Or written
down. Thoughts left unknown sentences unfin…
this world left behind. family, friends, strangers
only have my image in their memory.

What will they think? I was an average person? Were they
Left unmoved, unaffected, unimpressed? Would I
be just another book that would only be touched by
Dust? Or did they notice the colors in the sky even
When the sun set on my life? Will I be a framed
picture on the walls of their memory? Would my
beliefs even leave a dent in their mind? Or would I

Be too deep in their past to even recall my name?
Would I just be another girl that kept to herself?
Or was I a dandelion? Alive, bright yellow. Then
wild, gray, and free. Releasing seeds and creating
a cycle, a movement. Passing on what I left
behind. my spirit, my legacy. Whatever that may be?

How would they depict me? A dull portrait?
Little detail? Brown hair, brown eyes. Or every
Shade of my skin. will they remember the smile
I wore or the smiles I gave out? Or my heart's
Message to my loved ones? Will they remember
My silly moments or serious ones? Or will I be
Remembered at all? No one would care if a
Single leaf may fall. Just another human being.
Maybe it is pointless, wondering if I'll be remembered?

www.ingramcontent.com/pod-product-compliance
Lightning Source LLC
Chambersburg PA
CBHW042332150426
43194CB00001B/31